yl

M ... it the an ... ly to m ... onto- sau ... aying Ye ... e are creatures from Greek mythology, Scandinavian folklore and even John Bunyan and Shakespeare—all described in fast-moving humorous verse with delightful illustrations.

Charles Connell is a retired schoolmaster who has enjoyed writing poetry all his life. He has written many books, though this is his first children's title.

Please Ptell Me Pterodactyl

Charles Connell

Illustrated by John Millington

Beaver Books

First published in 1978 by
The Hamlyn Publishing Group Limited
London · New York · Sydney · Toronto
Astronaut House, Feltham, Middlesex, England

ISBN 0 600 36298 1

Printed in England by Cox and Wyman Limited
London, Reading and Fakenham
Set in Monotype Bembo

Contents

Introduction

Monsters Galore

There are monsters on the mountains,
There are monsters on the plains,
There are monsters in the sea and in the sky.
There are monsters in the city streets
And in the country lanes.
You can always find a monster if you try.

The scaly, spiny dinosaur
Lived in the swamps and bogs;
He was far too large to be a household pet.
He usually breakfasted
On unsuspecting frogs
Or on any other creatures he could get.

Although he was enormous,
Yet his skull was very small,
Which accounted for his rather tiny brain.
And it's really very sad to think
A beast so big and tall
Hadn't sense enough to come in from the rain.

He persuaded pterodactyls
To teach him how to fly,
But he flapped his artificial wings in vain,
And every time he failed
He gave a dinosauric sigh
And went back to the drawing board again.

But before he found the answer
To the mystery of flight,
Or realised he was heavier than air,
Every prehistoric monster
Said his ultimate goodnight,
Became extinct and simply wasn't there.

But the monster brood continued
And achieved a certain fame
In legend, myth and fable, fact and story.
And many will be dealt with,
Giving number, rank and name,
But we'll first set down a sort of inventory.

Any book of monster lore
Must include the Minotaur,
Apollyon, the Hydra and King Kong;
And no list would be complete
That ignored the Afreet,
Or the Jabberwock, the Wyvern, or the Dong.

It would be a pity if
We forgot the Hippogriff,
Or Briareus who had a hundred arms,
While we really can't refuse a
Tell-tale profile of Medusa,
A lady of most questionable charms.

Now the present writer thinks
The unfathomable Sphinx,
Like the Werewolf and the Roc, is truly quaint.

While the curious Unicorn
With his solitary horn,
If omitted, would have matter for complaint.

Then there's Polyphemus who
Well deserves a verse or two,
As does Griffin with its grotesque eagle's head.
Furthermore we'll try to fill a
Page or two about the Scylla,
And the Kraken rising from his watery bed.

Grendel, Argus, Cacus too
Are all waiting for their cue,
While Chimaera and the Boyg are sure to shock;
And we really mustn't risk
Leaving out the Basilisk,
Or the Scottish monster lurking in his loch.

All-in wrestler, Antaeus,
And three-headed Cerberus,
(Both beaten in fair fight by Hercules),
Drop in just to say 'Hello',
Like the dreaded Wendigo,
Mr Hyde and well-known monsters such as these.

There are many others too,
But we'll mention just a few –
Such as Dracula, the Yeti, Brontosaurus;
We'll permit ourselves a gag on
The adventures of the Dragon,
While Enceladus was simply tailored for us.

Not until I'd got them listed
Did I dream that there existed
Such a host of monsters, fictional or true;
But I hope that in some measure
My selection gives you pleasure.
If it does, I'll turn my hand to Volume Two!

1 Afreet

(Sometimes spelled Efreet or Afrit or Afrite, an understandably elusive monster from Mohammedan mythology.)

You can always spot an Afreet by his size;
If a ten-foot monster says he's one, he lies.
If his height is *fifty* feet,
He's too small for an Afreet.
You can always spot an Afreet by his size.

You can always tell an Afreet by his features;
He's the most repulsive of all monstrous creatures,
For the leer his face is set in
Makes him look just like a cretin.
You can always tell an Afreet by his features.

You will always know an Afreet by his ways
And the sheer maliciousness that he displays.
He tells filthy lies about you,
Making sure your friends all doubt you.
You will always know an Afreet by his ways.

You will recognise an Afreet by his laugh,
Like the shrill distinctive sneeze of a giraffe
Or a squealing leveret.
It's a sound you can't forget.
You will recognise an Afreet by his laugh.

You can always trace an Afreet by his smell,
Far from easy to define but *not* Chanel.
It's a sort of eastern pong
Reminiscent of Hong Kong.
You can always trace an Afreet by his smell.

Never try to catch an Afreet in a net.
It is something you will very soon regret.
Through the meshes he will squeeze
And demolish you with ease.
Never try to catch an Afreet in a net.

Never try to blow up Afreets in their lair,
For the odds are ten to one they just aren't there.
Far more likely they're behind you
And have neatly countermined you.
Never try to blow up Afreets in their lair.

Though the Afreet is unusually tall,
He can, if need be, make himself quite small,
So that when you think you've got him,
It's impossible to spot him
And you're forced to think he isn't there at all.

Once there *was* an Afreet tamed, I understand.
Old King Solomon, the wisest in the land,
Fixed him up in his harem,
Had him working like a dream,
But they say his concubines all lent a hand.

So I'm warning those who fancy an Afreet
Would be pleasant as a pet or good to eat,
No Afreet can with propriety
Mix with average society.
If you see one coming, beat a quick retreat.

2 Antaeus

(A formidable wrestling giant from Libya who was unbeatable until Hercules cleverly cut him off from his main source of strength – his mother, the earth goddess Ge.)

His mother was Queen of the Earth,
His father was King of the Sea;
So Antaeus's size
Caused no gasps of surprise,
Though his birth was a problem for Ge.

When Antaeus was only a child,
He stood fifty feet high in his socks.
One whole Stilton cheese
He could swallow with ease,
Washed down with the lightest of hocks.

As a youngster he found he could cope
With a hundred school meals every day.
When they said, 'That's enough',
He walked off in a huff.
'I refuse to start slimming,' he'd say.

His friends and relations agreed
He should go on a low calorie diet.
He asked, 'Does that include
A whole ox barbecued?
If it does, then I'm will to try it.'

His parents gave up in disgust,
For soon every cupboard was bare.
They just couldn't afford
To pay for his board;
Such arrangements, they said, were unfair.

He soon found his forte was wrestling –
Cross-buttock, back-breaker and whip –
His opponents would quail
And try to turn tail
When caught in his bone-crushing grip.

Any giant that came up against him
Would be broken in two like a stick.
All who watched were impressed,
For not one of them guessed
Every contest was won by a trick.

If Antaeus ever felt himself weakening,
To regain his full strength was no bother.
He pretended to swound,
Then lay flat on the ground
Till his batteries were recharged by Mother!

At last he received a new challenge
From the son of Alcmene and Zeus.
Hercules was his name;
He was destined for fame,
Very strong and by no means obtuse.

The previous night from the ringside
Hercules had been watching each fight,
And Antaeus he'd found
Started hugging the ground
Whenever defeat was in sight.

He remembered that Earth was the mother
Of Antaeus and straightway detected
That each time he fell,
The wrestler rose well
And stronger than might be expected.

So Hercules reached the conclusion
Antaeus was a fake and a sham.
While he lay there supine
And the count went to nine,
He was sucking up strength from his Mam!

So when Hercules met his opponent,
He lifted him up in the air
And he held him on high
Till his strength had run dry
And Antaeus was reduced to despair.

The spectators applauded and whistled
And jeered at Antaeus's plight.
When his face turned quite blue,
Every wrestling fan knew
It would soon be the end of the fight.

Remorselessly Hercules squeezed him,
His grip became tighter and crisper,
Till the giant all hated
Was fully deflated
And died not with a bang but a whisper.

Now the moral we draw from this story
Proves it really is better by far,
Whether page-boy or king,
To do one's own thing
And not to rely on one's Ma.

3 Apollyon

(*The evil angel of the bottomless pit who appears in Bunyan's* Pilgrim's Progress.)

From the day that he was weaned
People called him 'the foul fiend';
Winning Ugly Monster contests for his forte.
He'd a pair of dragon's wings,
Fishes' scales and other things,
And his conduct was particularly naughty.

That his feet were like a bear's
Was the source of lots of stares,
And his lion's mouth attracted much attention.
From his belly, too, there came
Clouds of smoke and tongues of flame
That shot out from places I don't care to mention.

Pilgrim's Progress is the book
Where Apollyon baits his hook
In the hope of catching Christian on the hop.
He was skilled in all the arts,
But excelled himself at darts
And the finish he preferred was 'double-top'.

He was lurking in an alley
In Humiliation's valley
With a set of brand-new 'arrows' in his hand.
He was spoiling for a fight,
So when Christian came in sight,
Apollyon commanded him to stand.

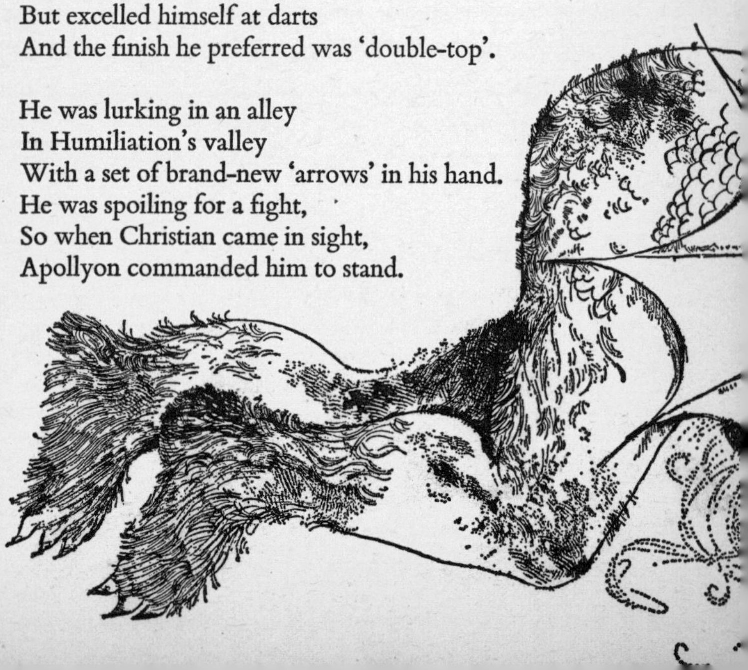

He bestrode the narrow track
And urged Christian to go back
To the place where he was born, Destruction City.
Chris, who'd had a premonition
The town was due for demolition,
Was convinced that to return would be a pity.

So the monster he ignored
And he grasped his two-edged sword,
Held his red-cross shield up to protect his skull.
On one issue he was clear –
He would *not* present his rear
Lest Apollyon should register a bull.

Then began a dreadful fight
Which went on into the night
And though badly wounded Christian would not yield.
Knowing it was hit or bust,
Christian gave one final thrust
That compelled his horrid foe to quit the field.

Now that valley desolate
Where Apollyon met his fate
Is haunted every night, (and day as well).
There's no phantom, so they say,
But men know he's been that way
By the ghastly, ghostly, foully fishy smell!

4 Argus

(The hundred-eyed monster employed by Hera to keep watch over her rival, Io.)

Of all the monsters men have known, the one to beat them all
Was Argus who possessed a hundred eyes,
But how they were distributed the stories don't recall;
We know nothing of their colour, shape or size.

Were they spaced out quite at random or arranged in tidy rows?
Did each optic operate in isolation?
Or did they do their work in pairs, either side a separate nose,
Or in any other curious combination?

Were they narrow slits or saucers? Were they laughing? Were
 they sad?
Were they blue or brown or black or grey or green?
Were they brimming with intelligence or glitteringly mad?
Were they icy, sympathetic, dull or keen?

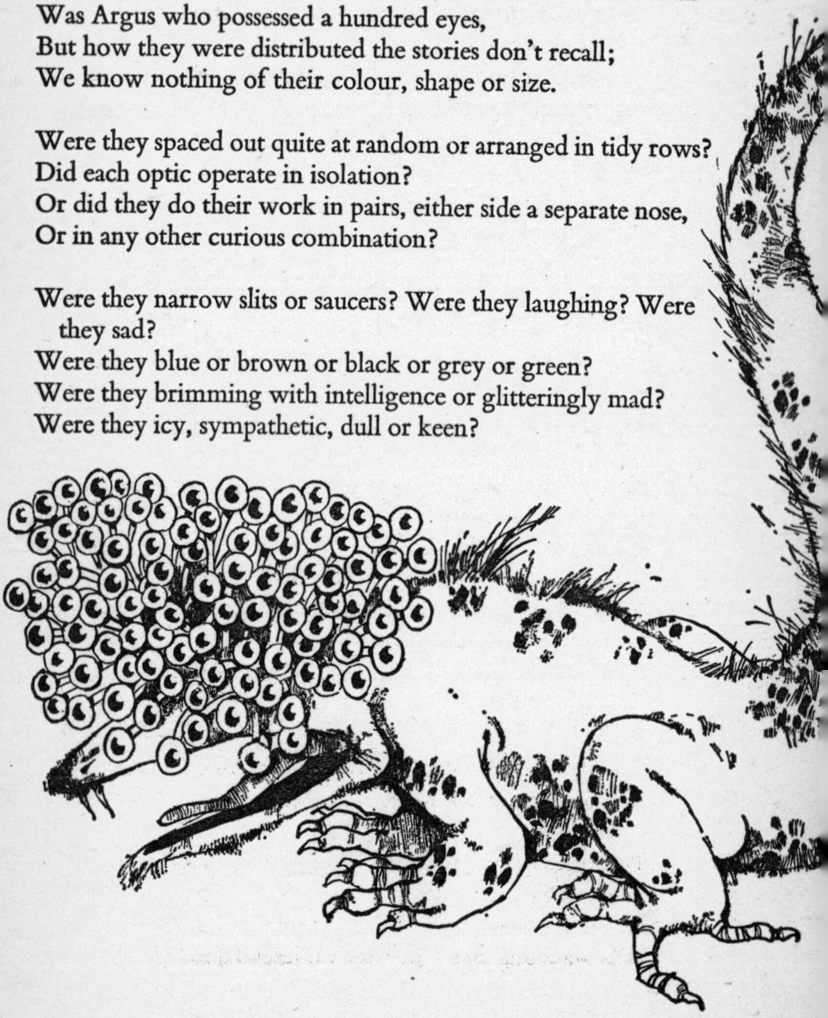

Oh, it used to be a moving sight whenever Argus wept;
All non-swimmers pleaded with him to desist.
On the other hand, imagine the confusion when he kept
An appointment with the family oculist.

There's one thing about the giant that nobody can deny –
He certainly had panoramic vision;
So when the goddess Hera thought she'd use a 'private eye',
She very quickly came to a decision.

She suspected that her husband Zeus was meeting on the sly
A young lady known as Io, quite a raver,
With whom he went out dancing in a country club near by.
(Hera looked upon this friendship with disfavour.)

Zeus's various flirtations were just driving Hera mad;
She was on the point of going home to mother,
But then she thought if evidence could be discreetly had,
A quick divorce would surely be less bother.

That she promptly sent for Argus will occasion no surprise;
He was obviously tailored for the task.
How could Zeus avoid being spotted by a hundred watchful
eyes?
Is the question you immediately ask.

As might have been expected, Zeus steered clear of all
romance
Till he thought that Hera trusted him once more.
Then one evening he took Io to a sort of dinner-dance
At a restaurant he'd never used before.

They danced rumba, fox-trot, tango, even did a palais glide.
Zeus assumed that they were safe from observation,
But in the building opposite, Argus, the hundred-eyed,
Was watching every move with fascination.

Later on, when Zeus discovered who had dropped him in the mire,
He ruthlessly put Argus on the spot.
He gave the job to Hermes, the inventor of the lyre,
Who assured him 'Hundred-Eyes' had had his lot.

Now Hermes was a trigger-man of cunning and finesse,
But each time he got near Argus he was spotted.
With his ranging vision Argus wasn't easy of access
In spite of all the schemes that Hermes plotted.

Then he called to mind that Argus was a sucker for a tune.
Marches thrilled him, while a torch song made him cry;
He responded to the lute, the flute, the fiddle, the bassoon,
But best of all he loved a lullaby.

So one night beneath his window Hermes strummed his tuneful
  lyre.
Then he gargled and began to improvise
A dreamy air that acted like a potent stupifier
And caused Argus to close *all* his hundred eyes.

Hermes just kept right on playing till he heard a tell-tale snore,
Then he quietly climbed the stairs towards his prey.
He found the room and tiptoed in and crept across the floor.
How he did the deed's a mystery to this day.

All we know is, thanks to Hermes, Argus hit the final trail,
But according to a story that I've heard,
His eyes live on, for Hera put them in the peacock's tail,
The peacock being Hera's sacred bird.

So if you should ever wonder why the peacock is so proud,
You can tell yourself his self-esteem is merited.
He's the only cock bird of the lot to stand out in a crowd
With the hundred tail-lights that he has inherited!

5 Basilisk

(A fabulous African reptile, hatched by a serpent from a cock's egg, whose glance and breath were supposed to be fatal.)

Of all the monsters known to man
Avoid at all times, if you can,
The Basilisk who creeps about
And manages to knock you out
Now with a look, now with his breath,
A crafty way to deal out death.

His birth, if all accounts be true,
At least deserves a line or two.
A cock bird's egg (though cocks don't lay)
Hatched by a serpent, so they say,
At last went pop and out there came
A Basilisk with eyes aflame.

His head and wings and web-shaped feet
Were like a cock's, as was most meet,
His tail was barbed and razor-keen,
More dangerous than the guillotine,
His breath was foul, as I have said,
And with a look he'd cut you dead.

My Uncle George of hunting fame
Had slaughtered every kind of game
From pheasant to rhinoceros;
The nimble hare, the albatross,
The tiger, panther, lynx and leopard,
Not counting beaters he had peppered.

But Uncle George was not content
And that is why he packed his tent,
His sleeping bag, some dynamite,
His gun (with telescopic sight),
And quite prepared to take the risk,
Went out to bag a Basilisk.

He said his prayers and then set forth.
He travelled south, he travelled north,
He journeyed east, he journeyed west
Upon his dedicated quest.
He went as far as Timbuctoo,
But not a Basilisk in view.

He pitched his camp in many a land,
On frozen waste, on burning sand,
In ferny forest, field and fen,
In darksome cave, in haunted glen.
In short, he hunted everywhere,
But Basilisks were never there.

If George was on a certain spot,
The wary Basilisk was not;
If he was told the address of one,
When he arrived the brute had gone;
No matter where he went to look,
The Basilisk had slung its hook.

For twenty years or more, I guess,
My Uncle searched without success;
Then gained a piece of information
That really filled him with elation.
The Basilisk, it seemed, could be
Attacked on two fronts, if not three.

A weasel, everyone declared,
Had Basilisks completely scared;
And then the crowing of the cock
Could deal the creatures quite a shock;
But best of all a looking-glass
Was sure to give the *coup de grâce.*

So Uncle launched a fresh attack.
He popped a weasel in a sack,
Encaged a lusty chanticleer,
Dumped all his military gear,
And when he marched into the field,
The bathroom mirror was his shield.

The second quest on which he went
Was tactically different.
Instead of rushing to and fro,
Hoping a Basilisk would show,
This time he stayed in one position
And fought a battle of attrition.

For George had heard that, come what might,
Perhaps by day, perhaps by night,
All worldly creatures, willy-nilly,
Were bound to pass by Piccadilly.
And so he lurked where Regent Street
And crowded Piccadilly meet.

His patience was rewarded when
One Friday morning just at ten
He saw a Basilisk at last
From Coventry Street approaching fast,
And on its face a dreadful leer.
Uncle was petrified with fear.

He soon recovered from the shock
And when his knees had ceased to knock,
Though everybody else had fled,
He held his mirror overhead,
Behaving with great circumspection,
And eyed the Basilisk's reflection.

He watched the crafty beast's advance
And then my Uncle took a chance,
Released the weasel from its sack
And set it on the creature's track;
Then loosed the cock which straight away
Crowed lustily to greet the day.

The Basilisk, brought to a halt
By this surprise combined assault,
Chilled by the weasel's beady eyes
And deafened by the cock's shrill cries,
Gripped by the icy hand of terror,
Fell into fundamental error.

Unable to resist temptation,
He gazed with horrid fascination
At Uncle's mirror held on high,
And transfixed by the evil eye
Of his reflection, stared aghast,
Staggered, collapsed, then breathed his last.

Historical accounts record
That Uncle reaped his due reward.
First as Sir George he made his name,
But later tasted real fame
When nominated by the Crown
Lord Basilisk of London Town.

6 Boyg

(A vague troll-monster, impalpable and invulnerable, which belongs to Norwegian folk-lore and appears in Ibsen's Peer Gynt.)

The Boyg is quite invisible;
That's why I've never spotted one.
It also is impregnable;
That's why I've never potted one.
They say, too, it's impalpable;
That's why I've never handled one.
It never was a baby
And so I've never dandled one.

I know the Boyg's invulnerable;
I've certainly not beaten one.
Moreover it's inedible;
Therefore I've never eaten one.
Of course the Boyg's unmailable;
That's why I've never posted one.
I heard it's uninflammable;
Small wonder I've not roasted one.

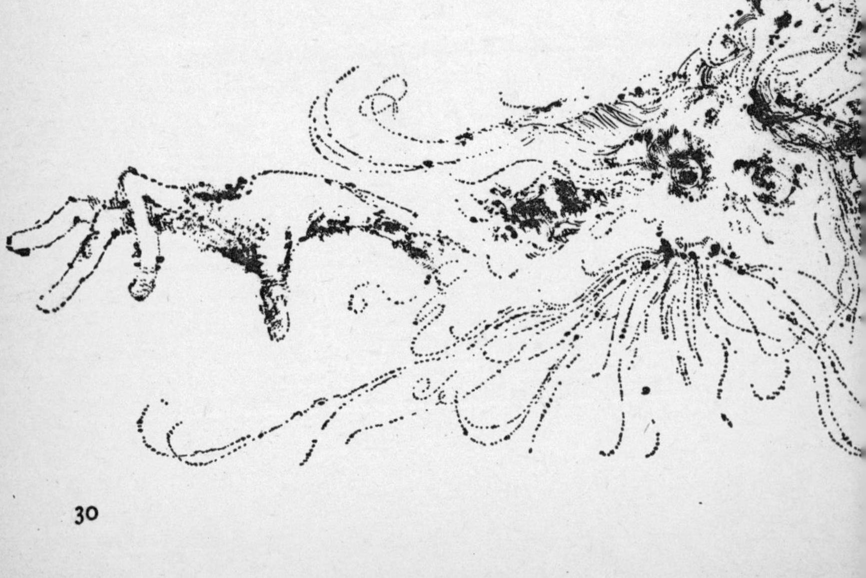

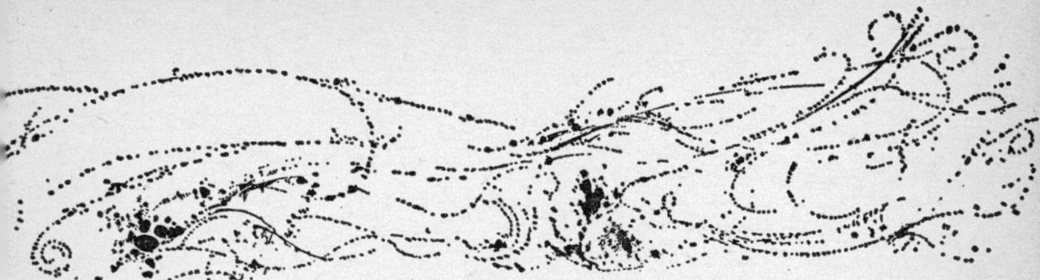

It's true the Boyg's imponderable;
Don't try to guess the weight of one.
Besides, it's unpredictable,
So don't foretell the fate of one.
No doubt it's inaccessible,
So never try to get at one.
It's temper's irrepressible,
So never make a friend of one.

The facts about the Boyg appear
To be completely negative.
We seek him there, we seek him here;
Our approach is purely tentative.
If you'd know more of this Troll-King,
Then here's a useful hint:
I suggest that you start walking
In the footsteps of Peer Gynt.

7 Briareus

(A giant in Greek mythology who possessed a hundred hands and fifty heads.)

Briareus was a Titan
Who fought against the gods.
He never was defeated,
No matter what the odds.

It's really not surprising
He always won each fight.
With fifty heads and a hundred arms
He looked a shocking sight.

With his heads he worked out strategy –
All giants were impressed.
From fifty possible battle plans
He always chose the best.

His hundred arms proved useful
In every kind of brawl.
When he flung a hundred punches,
You couldn't dodge them all.

He and his brother giants
Of various shapes and sizes
Chased all the gods to Egypt,
Where they lurked in many guises.

The first of all the routed gods
To take it on the lam
Was Jupiter, who assumed the form
And features of a ram.

Bacchus became a billy-goat
And Mercury a bird,
While Venus changed into a fish
And looked somewhat absurd.

Diana turned into a cat,
Apollo was a crow.
Briareus roared with laughter
When he saw them in a row.

He mocked them with his fifty mouths,
Treating them with disdain,
But poked most fun at Jupiter;
Just why I can't explain.

But Jupiter still had a shot
In the Olympian locker,
A secret weapon specially made
To use against the mocker.

Minerva made some thunderbolts
For Jupiter, who said
To Vulcan, 'Keep on firing them
Till Briareus is dead.'

Vulcan's initial volley
Was packed with dynamite,
For twenty heads flew right to left
And twenty left to right.

He lowered his sights and tried again,
Once more his aim was true,
And fifty of Briareus's arms
Were blown to Timbuctoo.

The third and final salvo
Did everything that mattered.
The giant's remaining heads and legs
About the field were scattered.

They cremated poor Briareus,
As was only fair and just.
They needed seventeen rows of urns
To house the giant's dust!

8 Brontosaurus

(A giant lizard belonging to the dinosaur family and possibly sixty-five feet (nearly twenty metres) in length.)

The Brontosaurus, as you know,
Lived many, many years ago,
Roaming the prehistoric swamp,
Rheumaticky because of damp,
Sleeping by night, hunting by day,
Eating whatever came his way.
Some sixty feet from nose to tail;
His hide was like a coat of mail.

Because he weighed a ton or so
His movements were extremely slow.
His speed, when using all his power,
Rarely attained three miles an hour.
He tried in many a minor race,
But always failed to gain a place;
Yet even in that age Jurassic
He often longed to win a classic.

He thought about the situation
And after much deliberation
Decided that his steady pace
Was best for a long-distance race.
'The Dinosauric Leger might
Turn out,' he said, 'exactly right.
The Guineas is too fast for me;
The Derby's not my cup of tea.'

Each day in every kind of weather
He and his trainer got together
And galloped round the countryside
From early morn till eventide.
His speed increased with every pace
And, confident he'd win the race,
He said, 'If I maintain this, I'll
Achieve the fifteen-minute mile!'

And then at length the great day came
When he set out to make his name
In Doncaster, a northern town
Of grand and glorious renown,
Where the first Leger had its birth
In the beginnings of the earth.
Almost two miles had to be run
To find the annual champion.

Huge dinosaurs of every sort,
All eager to enjoy the sport,
To Doncaster had made their way
Upon this memorable day.
The inns were full; all stables booked;
Great dinosauric meals were cooked,
For every pleasure-loving beast
Turned up for this historic feast.

All entrants for the Leger Plate
Assembled at the starting gate,
The Brontosaurus looked around
And then began to paw the ground.
No brontosauri were in sight.
Iguanodons to left and right
Made up the field, with just one grey
Diplodocus from the U.S.A.

Down went the starter's flag at last
And off they galloped, very fast,
Thundering along at breakneck speed.
(Diplodocus was in the lead.)
With seven furlongs still to go
The race was clearly touch and go.
Diplodocus would win, they reckoned,
With Brontosaurus lying second.

With less than fifty yards to run,
Diplodocus was almost done.
The Brontosaurus, slightly fresher,
Decided to put on the pressure,
And suddenly gave such a bound
That like a bird he left the ground.
He closed his eyes and swelled with pride;
He'd never had a smoother ride.

His take-off had been really tops;
His landing was the worst of flops,
Flat on his belly, legs a-sprawl;
Never did pride have such a fall.
But he was luckier than most;
He did this near the winning post,
And when he crashed down on the deck,
The judges yelled, 'Won by a neck!'

Having achieved his one ambition,
He withdrew from all competition.
His fellow dinosaurs agreed
They had no further use for speed.
They found that life was too complex,
Degenerated into wrecks,
And long before the Cave Man blinked
They gradually became extinct.

9 Bully Bottom

(*The play-acting weaver in Shakespeare's* A Midsummer Night's Dream *who was 'translated' into a monster when Puck gave him an ass's head.*)

I wasn't a monster for long,
So don't class me with Dong or King Kong,
Or with Yeti or Yahoo,
Or Hydra or Rahu,
For I wasn't a monster for long.

I'll tell you just how it fell out
And my tale you've no reason to doubt.
It began with a play
For the Duke's wedding day,
With Quince, Starveling, Flute, Snug and Snout.

The six of us went in a wood
Near Athens – we rehearsed where we could –
I had the main part
And, joking apart,
The other five weren't very good.

Our play concerned Thisbe and P.,
Meaning Pyramus, acted by me.
We had to rely on
Poor Snug for the Lion,
But he wouldn't have frightened a flea.

Robin Starveling as Moon broke your heart;
His lantern went out for a start.
He came in with a rush
And tripped over a bush,
And fluffed every line of his part.

Concealed by the trunk of a yew,
I was waiting to hear my cue,
When a creature called Puck
Unexpectedly struck
And fashioned my features anew.

He made my own head disappear,
(I assure you it felt very queer!)
And he gave me instead
A complete ass's head.
'Twas the quickest transplant of the year.

When I entered to make my first speech,
Thisbe uttered a falsetto screech
And set out like the wind,
With the rest close behind,
To put themselves well out of reach.

I started to carol a ditty,
So poignant, yet tuneful and witty.
It was all about birds;
I've forgotten the words.
Every one will agree that's a pity.

My song awoke Oberon's Queen,
A fairy of exquisite mien.
She looked into my eyes
And said, 'Apart from your size,
You're the handsomest fellow I've seen.'

Four fairies fulfilled every need –
Cobweb, Peaseblossom, Moth, Mustardseed.
Two sat scratching my head,
While the other two said
They would bring me my favourite feed.

The Queen stroked my ears and my nose;
It was love at first sight, I suppose.
She sang lullabies
And I closed both my eyes,
For I felt in the mood for a doze.

Then I slumbered, and when I awoke
I found it had all been a joke.
I'd got back my own head,
My wee Queenie had fled
And so had the four fairy folk.

So I wasn't a monster for long;
All I did was sing one little song,
Found my face had turned hairy,
Fell in love with a fairy,
But I didn't do anything wrong.

And if you would learn my technique,
How to woo, (though a bit of a freak),
Book a seat at our play
On the Duke's wedding-day.
(Twice nightly the rest of the week.)

10 Cacus

(A thieving giant who lived in a cave on Mount Aventine and who plundered the countryside until he was slain by Hercules.)

Cacus was a monster,
Cacus was a thief;
He stole a herd of cattle,
(An awful lot of beef!)
They once belonged to Geryon
Whom Hercules had fought
And polished off and plundered.
(So classicists are taught.)

Now Cacus had been crafty
When he knocked off the herd;
He grabbed their tails and dragged them
(Though this may seem absurd)
Backwards across the country
And hid them in his lair,
So Hercules went hunting
For a trail that wasn't there.

The cattle tracks all led him
To where the herd had been
When Cacus did his rustling,
Then nothing more was seen.
Poor Hercules was baffled;
He could only stand and stare.
It seemed as if the cattle
Had vanished in thin air.

But then in desperation
He went back along the trail,
Which led him to Mount Aventine,
(According to the tale)
And as he passed the cavern
He was suddenly aware
Of a melancholy lowing,
So he knew the herd was there.

Without a word of warning,
Our hero strode inside,
Knocked the stuffing out of Cacus,
(Justifiable homicide!)
He carved on the giant's head-stone,
(You can see it to this day),
This admonitory message –
Cattle rustling doesn't pay!

11 Cerberus

(Pluto's three-headed dog that was responsible for guarding the gates of Hell.)

Some dogs like to hunt the fox,
While others chase the hare;
Some dogs are unorthodox
And other dogs are square.

Some dogs sit before the fire;
Others prefer the street.
Some dogs gimble, others gyre,
Some won't touch potted meat.

Some dogs do nothing else but bark;
Other dogs merely wheeze.
Some go for 'walkies' in the park;
Some have long pedigrees.

Most people like the doggy race,
Both gentlemen and ladies,
But the one dog that they cannot face
Is Cerberus from Hades.

This famous watch-dog guards the gate
That leads straight down to Hell.
One finds it hard to concentrate
When caught within its spell.

The three heads of this curious beast
Create an odd impression.
Three mouths and sixty teeth at least
Suggest distinct aggression.

Six eyes, three throats, a triple bark,
And serpent's tail to boot
Are surely worthy of remark
In any four-legged brute.

This cunning monster wagged its tail
When new arrivals came,
But still the creature without fail
Would bite them just the same.

He'd bite you when you entered Hell,
But then he'd hang about
And tear to pieces, legends tell,
All those who wanted out.

Now Hercules was, (as you knew),
Always performing labours,
Like stealing girdles, apples too.
(Disturbing for the neighbours.)

One memorable laborious day,
Part of his daily round
Was down to Hades make his way
And come back with the hound.

He grabbed it here, he grabbed it there,
Dodging its triple bite;
Then swung it up into the air,
Holding throats left and right.

It barked and howled and snapped and tore,
But Hercules just waited
Till Cerberus could fight no more,
Completely subjugated.

Eventually he sent it back
To guard the gates of hell.
Gone were the looks demoniac
Of Hades' sentinel.

That little brush with Hercules
Had left the beast quite tame;
It simply sprawled there at its ease
Impervious to shame.

All those condemned to go below
After life's earthly span
Find Cerberus gentle, friendly, slow
And vegetarian.

So don't let destiny disturb
You on the final trail.
Just knock three times and ask for Cerb;
He'll grin and wag his tail!

12 Chimaera

(A legendary Greek monster with a lion's head, goat's body and dragon's tail who was killed by Bellerophon.)

The Chimaera, says the legend,
Was a crazy mixed-up beast;
Lion, dragon, goat compounded,
Typically Middle-East.

Front-end lion, middle goat-like,
Rear-end of a raging dragon.
Confirmed drinkers, if they saw one,
Straight away went on the wagon.

Born of Typhon and Echidna,
The Chimaera was the end.
Even similar Chimaeras
Would not have him as a friend.

He was ravaging Lycia
And all kingdoms round about.
Many Greeks had tried to kill him,
But he put them all to rout.

To the court of Iobates
Galloped bold Bellerophon,
Recommended by King Proetus
In a really royal 'con'.

For King Proetus had suspicions
That his wife was having fun
At the royal garden parties
With the young Bellerophon.

So he sent his cunning rival
To Lycia with a note
Offering gold to Iobates
If he'd cut the young man's throat.

But the wily Iobates,
(Most reluctant trigger-man),
Far from keen to do a murder,
Found a way to pass the can.

He resolved to stage a contest,
With a prize for him who won,
'Twixt the three-in-one Chimaera
And the lone Bellerophon.

So no matter what the outcome,
Iobates couldn't lose.
He was bound to please *one* party;
Only destiny could choose.

If Bellerophon was slaughtered,
He would reap his just reward
From King Proetus; if Chimaera
Died, all Lycians would applaud.

Bellerophon, though young, was crafty;
He knew strength was not enough.
Outside aid was surely needed
'Gainst an enemy so tough.

So he borrowed from Minerva
Pegasus, the horse that flew;
Promptly leaped into the saddle,
Rocketed into the blue.

Soon he spotted the Chimaera
Basking in the noonday sun,
Unaware that up above him
Soared a flying stallion.

Bellerophon then dug his spurs in,
Gave the wonder horse his head.
Down he swooped as fast as lightning.
The monster was as good as dead.

Guided by his skilful rider,
Pegasus then checked his flight,
Hovered over the Chimaera
Who was too surprised to fight.

Two swift strokes were soon delivered,
Through the air the sharp blade dropped.
Into three distinctive sections
The Chimaera then was chopped.

One part lion, one part dragon,
One part goat – and all parts bled,
And thus ended the Chimaera,
For each separate part was dead!

13 Dinosaur

(An extinct reptile of tremendous size. The name means 'terror-lizard'.)

Ten awkward dinosaurs marching in a line;
One tripped and broke his neck: then there were nine.

Nine clumsy dinosaurs trying hard to skate;
One crashed right through the ice: then there were eight.

Eight gawky dinosaurs hitch-hiking through Devon;
One got lost on Dartmoor: then there were seven.

Seven bungling dinosaurs, keen on magic tricks;
One was *really* sawn in half: then there were six.

Six feckless dinosaurs learning how to dive;
One put no water in the tank: then there were five.

Five warlike dinosaurs joined the recce corps;
One couldn't read a map: then there were four.

Four reckless dinosaurs sailing on the sea;
A hungry shark swallowed one: then there were three.

Three demented dinosaurs in search of Doctor Who;
One argued with a Dalek: then there were two.

Two enterprising dinosaurs explored the Amazon;
One trod on a crocodile: then there was one.

One lonely dinosaur, when all his friends had gone,
Simply pined away and died: then there was none.

14 Dong

(A lonely wild creature, invented by Edward Lear, that has a luminous nose and haunts 'the great Gromboolian plain'.)

The Dong is not the sound you get
By hammering a gong to let
The family know it's time to start a meal;
It's not the deep reverberant roar
Of angry wave upon the shore;
It's not the echoing ring of iron on steel.

And when the average citizen,
In trying to describe Big Ben,
Declares each stroke reminds him of a Dong,
We view his notions with concern
And hope that he will quickly learn
Comparisons can sometimes be quite wrong.

The Dong, (the experts all agree),
Was a simple fellow just like me,
Who used to roam the great Gromboolian plain.
He played his pipe or sang gay songs,
Exactly like his fellow Dongs
Who thought him gentle, sensible and sane.

And then, alas, it's sad to say,
He met a Jumbly Girl one day
And loved the dainty creature to distraction.
In the beginning all was bliss,
But later on the fickle miss
Fell out of love and took evasive action.

She went down to the water side
And launched a sieve and leaped inside.
She set her sail; the day was bright and breezy.
And then she realised her mistake –
She had to bale without a break.
(To keep a sieve afloat's by no means easy!)

Treated so scurvily by Fate,
The Dong was quite disconsolate
And turned into a monster overnight.
He prowled the plain, the fields, the shore;
He'd howl and shriek and rave and roar,
And spread alarm, despondency and fright.

And as the weeks crept slowly by,
The more he tried to horrify,
Employing techniques never used before.
His brother Dongs shook at the knees
And wisely stayed in twos and threes
From Zemmery Fidd down to the Chankly Bore.

As every well-read reader knows,
The Dong dreamed up a dummy nose,
A huge one woven from the Twangum Tree.
He made it from the Twangum's bark
And wore it only after dark:
At sight of it the boldest Dong would flee.

He painted it a vivid red
And in its end, so people said,
He fixed a lamp that shot out lurid rays;
And as he wandered to and fro,
His nose gave off a fiery glow;
All of his face, in fact, appeared to blaze.

And that is how the story goes
About the Dong's peculiar nose,
But I don't think his motive was to scare.
He prowled at night along the shore
From Zemmery Fidd to Chankly Bore
To find the girl who'd given him the air!

15 Dracula

(A Romanian count and vampire who appeared in the novel Dracula *by Bram Stoker.)*

You may find them in Albania,
But your best bet's Transylvania,
Where they flitter and they flutter through the night.
If you track one to its lair,
I suggest you take great care
And refuse if it should offer you a bite.

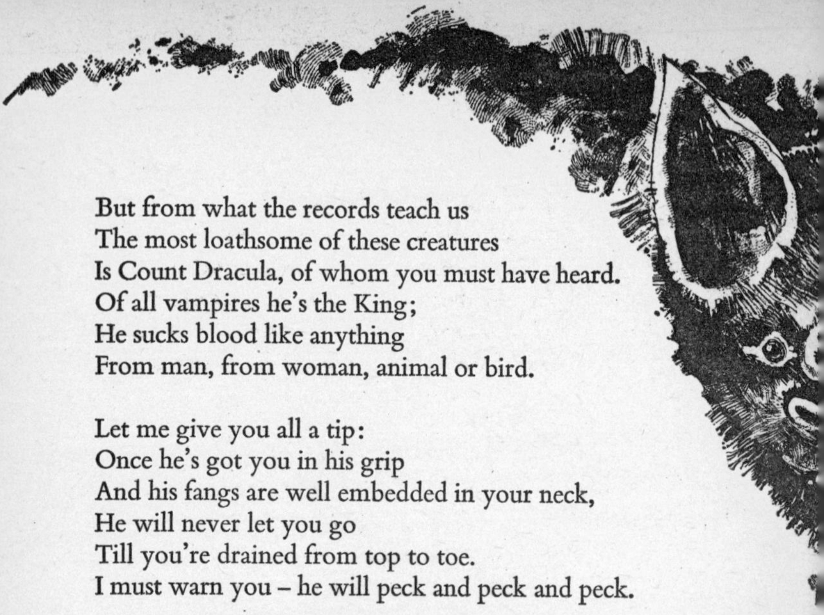

But from what the records teach us
The most loathsome of these creatures
Is Count Dracula, of whom you must have heard.
Of all vampires he's the King;
He sucks blood like anything
From man, from woman, animal or bird.

Let me give you all a tip:
Once he's got you in his grip
And his fangs are well embedded in your neck,
He will never let you go
Till you're drained from top to toe.
I must warn you – he will peck and peck and peck.

You can't keep him out at all;
He can walk up any wall
And he simply laughs all bars and bolts to scorn.
He will wait till you're asleep,
Then into your room he'll creep
And if he's in the vein, he'll drink till dawn.

In my many learned chats
With my friends on vampire bats,
I've picked up a lot of useful information;
So if you should ever hear
That Count Dracula is near,
My advice will help in such a situation.

Garlic bunched in pungent spray
Will protect you night and day
If distributed round door and window frames.
Dracula can't stand the stuff
And one whiff is quite enough
To persuade him to postpone his little games.

I have also heard folks say
That he rests throughout the day
And sleeps inside a coffin in a crypt.
You can thump him, you can shake him,
But you never will awake him.
'I'm a *bloody* heavy sleeper!' he once quipped.

If you're hoping to dispatch him,
That's the time you've got to catch him,
(And please don't rely on bullets or cold steel).
If he isn't sound asleep,
You may tiptoe, you may creep,
But he'll slip away as easily as an eel.

You can choke him, you can eat him,
But the only way to beat him
Is with crucifix and consecrated wafer.
Keep a cross beside your bed
And a slice of well-blessed bread,
Then you're bound to feel considerably safer.

My advice, for what it's worth,
If you run the Count to earth,
Is to act without the slightest hesitation.
Grab a hammer for a start
And drive a stake right through his heart,
Then follow up with swift decapitation.

If you're ever on your own,
Without friend or chaperon,
And a stranger's prowling round the neighbourhood;
If he says he's feeling dry
And can't look you in the eye,
It's Count Dracula a-thirsting for your blood!

16 Dragon

(Dragons came in many shapes and sizes. The one here described is the dragon that terrorised the inhabitants of Silene until it was slain by St George, England's patron saint.)

Although we look upon Saint George as England's patron saint,
Don't ever call him Englishman, 'cos that's just what he ain't.
Though men in England all agree no patron saint is finer,
They never hide the fact that George was born in Asia Minor.

Saint Patrick for the Irishman, Saint Andrew for the Scot,
Saint David for the Welshman must never be forgot;
Saint James is for the Spaniard, but in England it is certain
Born further east George might have been behind the Iron
Curtain!

We English are romantics and our fancies wander free,
Especially when dealing with Saint George's family tree,
But our chroniclers will tell you there's one story that is true;
He *really* slew a dragon and I'll tell the tale to you.

In a lake outside Silene a huge dragon used to dwell;
It ate all the people's rations and then turned on them as well.
It would swallow them for breakfast, dinner, tea and even supper,
Washing down each generous mouthful with a truly tasty 'cuppa'.

Every night the dragon ravaged, grabbing victims for the pot,
Chewed them up and spat the bones out, well contented with his
lot.
All the people in the district didn't dare to go to bed,
For they never could be certain that the Dragon had been fed.

Then the wise men of the city hit upon a crafty scheme,
Put it into operation and it worked just like a dream.
In a field outside the city walls they left two sheep each day
And the Dragon came and gulped them down, then quietly went
away.

Everything was running smoothly till they ran right out of sheep,
So the Dragon paid a visit while the folks were fast asleep.
As a sign of his displeasure he ate half-a-dozen earls,
Seven seneschals, a herald, two fat pages, three plump girls.

Thereupon the City Fathers finalised a second plan
Which included everybody – girl and woman, boy and man.
All their names on scraps of paper went in a revolving drum.
One was drawn each day and that one ended in the Dragon's tum.

All except the luckless victim found the system worked all right.
No more cowering in cellars, no disturbances at night.
The Dragon, too, was satisfied, for when it came to meat,
'Twas human flesh, (arm, leg or rump), that he preferred to eat.

And so for many months the daily round went with a swing
Until one day the lot fell on the daughter of the King.
Poor Princess Saba's name was drawn and there was no appeal;
Fate dictated that the girl would be the Dragon's evening meal.

Saba put on her Sunday best and wore her golden crown
And waited in the appointed place a mile outside the town.
She prayed to all the gods above and heaved a woeful sigh.
She thought the end was near, but then Saint George came
riding by.

He asked her why she looked so sad and Saba said that Fate
Had destined her to ornament the Dragon's dinner plate.
Trussed like a chicken, neatly stuffed, served medium or rare,
She'd figure with French Fried upon the Dragon's bill of fare.

Saint George said, 'By my halidom! Nay! Fol-di-diddle-dee!
Just stand behind yon hawthorn hedge and leave the rest to me.'
The Princess did as she was bid and tried hard to relax,
While George took practice swings and thrusts with lance and
battle-axe.

A twelve-foot weapon, George declared, gave him a better chance
And consequently he resolved to use his trusty lance.
He leaped upon his milk-white steed, down to the lake he rode
Wherein the hated Dragon had his watery abode.

Not waiting for the dinner gong, the hungry beast appeared,
Gave one glance at his foe and then contemptuously sneered.
He opened his cavernous mouth and shot out tongues of fire
Which, licking fiercely round Saint George, compelled him to retire.

The Saint pulled down his helmet to protect him from the heat,
Buckled his armour tighter and crouched low in his seat.
Holding his lance before him, he then took careful aim,
And clinging to his horse's mane charged through the smoke and flame.

A foot or more the lance went through the Dragon's scaly breast.
Although 'twas not a death-blow, yet the creature gave him best.
The Princess joined them when she saw the Dragon was outclassed,
Unclasped her jewelled belt and quickly bound the monster fast.

Back they rode into the city, with the Dragon on a lead,
And the people praised their saviour for so valorous a deed.
As for George, he made them Christians, taught them to be kind and meek.
Taught them how to live together, how to turn the other cheek.

He gave a talk on love and goodness and on virtues such as those,
Urged them to be tender-hearted, urged them to forgive their foes,
Stressed that in a Christian country *all* God's creatures should be brothers,
Then he chopped the Dragon's head off as a warning to the others.

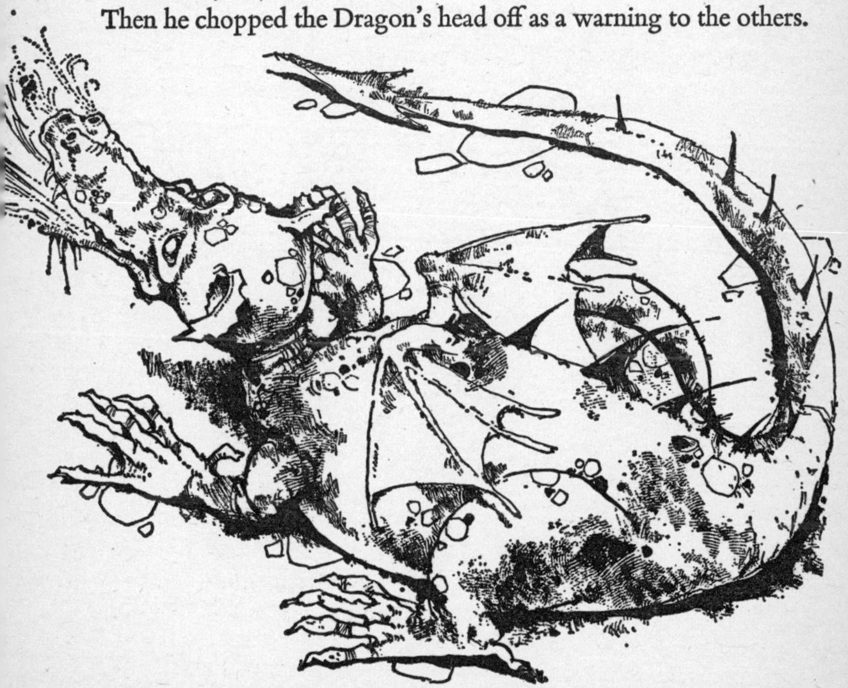

17 Enceladus

(A superhuman hundred-armed giant who made war on the gods, who was killed by Zeus and who was subsequently buried under Mount Etna.)

I don't know much, and that's a fact, about Enceladus,
Except that he was more than twice the size of Tityus,
And Tityus, the stories tell, when lying on a plain,
Covered at least six acres and half as much again.

Enceladus, then, must have been a giant easily noticed.
It irks me that he was ignored by every anecdotist,
And so I feel I must record his one claim to renown –
His body lies in Sicily; Mount Etna keeps it down!

18 Grendel

(A huge man-eating monster who patrolled the fens near the castle of the Danish King Hrothgar until it was slain by Beowulf.)

Of all the creatures men have seen,
Or here in the Might-Have-Been,
The ugliest monster of them all
Was one that ravaged Heorot Hall
And swallowed lots and lots of Danes –
Feet, legs and bodies, heads and brains.

His name was Grendel and his den
Was far away across a fen,
And there he used to sit and brood
On ways and means of getting food,
Preferring to eat human flesh,
Especially when it was fresh.

From time to time the beast would call
Upon the Danes of Heorot Hall,
Eating a dozen, sometimes more,
Scattering their bones about the floor,
And at each horrible repast
He kept the fattest till the last.

Hrothgar, the King, wept in his beard
As his best warriors disappeared.
And was so doleful and depressed,
He wrung his hands and beat his breast.
He sobbed and sighed, he peaked and pined,
But no solution could he find.

And then one day a ship arrived
And Hrothgar's spirits fast revived,
For the first one to disembark
Was Beowulf, a man of mark,
Who'd brought more monsters to their knees
Than the Greek hero, Hercules.

A royal feast was quickly planned
For Beowulf and his warrior band,
On that most memorable of nights
The Hall of Heorot blazed with lights,
And jesters jested, tumblers tumbled,
While many a noble belly rumbled.

And after all the revelry
Beowulf disclosed his strategy.
King Hrothgar and his Danes, he said,
Would be far better off in bed.
He and his men in fighting gear
Would wait for Grendel to appear.

Meanwhile far off across the fen
The monster, lurking in his den,
Had listened to the twanging lute,
The stirring drum, the piercing flute,
The harp, the fiddle, bones and tongs,
The laughter and the bawdy songs.

Incensed and maddened by it all
Grendel set out for Heorot Hall
To teach the Danes a lesson they
Would not forget for many a day.
He galloped all the way that night
Just to work up an appetite.

He reached the doors and knocked them flat,
Ignored the 'Welcome' on the mat,
And before Beowulf could get him
He grabbed a warrior and ate him,
Spat out some bones and hair and gore,
Then licked his lips and looked for more.

Now Beowulf as a little lad
Had starred in the Olympiad.
He'd fought in many a boxing ring;
As all-in wrestler he was king;
And all sports commentators knew
He was a master of Kung Fu.

Though Beowulf was big and strong,
It didn't take him very long
To hit upon a course of action
Most likely to give satisfaction.
To fight a beast of such a size
The finest weapon was surprise.

He waited until Grendel struck
And then his answer was to duck.
Grabbing the monster by the wrist,
He gave its arm a vicious twist
And forced it up behind its back
Until the shoulder-blade went crack!

Then Beowulf gave a mighty heave,
And though not easy to believe,
He tugged that arm with might and main,
Causing excruciating pain,
And yanked it off – and please don't laugh! –
He used it like a quarterstaff.

The monster was so pulverised,
So thoroughly demoralised,
That he ran back across the fen
And there took refuge in his den,
Living henceforth on frogs and newts,
On ragged reeds and rotting roots.

Never again, when Grendel dined,
Did he feast on the human kind,
While Hrothgar and his Danish men
Found him a model citizen,
And captivated by his charm,
They stuffed and gave him back his arm.

19 Griffin

(Sometimes spelled griffon or gryphon, this fabulous monster had the head and wings of an eagle and the body and hindquarters of a lion.)

One half of the Griffin's a mammal;
One half of the Griffin's a bird.
An odd mixture of lion and eagle,
The beast is grotesque and absurd.

Its ears are as long as a horse's,
Its wing-span is twenty-five feet,
In one claw it can carry two oxen
And that's a significant feat.

Its nest, lined with gold, is tremendous.
When broody it stands on one leg.
The back half of the Griffin is lion,
Which explains why it can't lay an egg.

If perchance you would study the Griffin,
I know where at least there is one –
In the arms of the City of London,
Quite rampant and ready for fun!

20 Hippogriff

(Offspring of a griffin and a mare, this curious beast was found in the more mountainous northern regions.)

Don't tell yourself you're dreaming if
You ever meet a Hippogriff.
The father, (demi-lion, half-eagle),
Mama a mare, (the union's legal!)
It's not surprising that their baby
Has mane, tail, wings, claws, feathers, maybe.
A most peculiar mutation
Deserves a fitting appellation,
So don't blame legend-makers if
They called the beast a Hippogriff.

21 Hyde

(The evil personality assumed by Doctor Jekyll under the influence of a drug he had discovered.)

I confess that I am baffled,
Lost, bewildered, mystified,
For one day he's Doctor Jekyll
And the next day Mr Hyde.

It's impossible to know him,
Though I reckon I have tried,
But he's sometimes Doctor Jekyll
And he's sometimes Mr Hyde.

Some who meet him find him charming,
Others are just terrified,
For he might be Doctor Jekyll
Or he could be Mr Hyde.

Sometimes you will really like him;
Sometimes you'll be horrified.
You can safely visit Jekyll,
But don't trust him when he's Hyde.

His behaviour when it's daylight
Can so easily misguide,
For at that time he is Jekyll,
But at night he's Mr Hyde.

He's all right from dawn till sunset;
After that he might backslide,
For he's finished being Jekyll
And it's welcome Mr Hyde.

When he's swallowed half a glassful,
Straightaway he's uglified
And the handsome Doctor Jekyll
Makes a most repulsive Hyde.

He sprouts hair in curious places
And looks strangely evil-eyed,
Once he's changed from Doctor Jekyll
To the wicked Mr Hyde.

If you ask about his problem,
His reply may be surmised.
'Though the money's good as Jekyll,
I get far more fun as Hyde!'

Most of us can change our natures,
But we never can decide
Whether to play safe as Jekyll
Or take a chance as Mr Hyde.

22 Hydra

(The many-headed monster slain by Hercules as one of his twelve labours.)

There has been a lot of argument about the Hydra's heads;
Some say this and some say that, no two agree.
Just how many heads she had
Almost drives the critics mad
And the reason is not difficult to see.

The problem with the Hydra was that chopping off one head
Only increased the confusion, let us face it,
For when one head was removed,
It was demonstrably proved
Two other heads would straight away replace it.

So counting heads was useless, even if the thing kept still,
But she didn't, she was always changing places.
She made wriggles, coils and squirms,
And her necks like giant worms
Balanced lots of leering hideous human faces.

One of Hercules' ten labours was to slay this curious beast,
So he went with Iolanus to Lake Lerna.
He said, 'First we'll try surprise;
After that we'll cauterise.
If we can't behead her, we must simply burn her!'

They found the Hydra splashing in the squishy squelchy marsh
Where the many-headed monster had her lair.
Swords sliced and slashed and wheeled,
But each severed neck soon healed
And for every head that rolled there grew a pair.

Our hero said, 'Iolanus, if we keep this up we're lost;
This beast's more dangerous than she was before.
She had fifty heads, I think;
Now, although we've fought like stink
On the latest count I make it ninety-four!'

Then Hercules decided it was time to try Plan 'B'.
Iolanus simply had to guard his rear.
So although the grass was wet,
With *The Athenian Gazette*
He lit a fire and heated up his spear.

Signalling to Iolanus to chop off another head,
The wily Greek rushed in with red-hot steel,
And in less than half a sec'
Plunged it in the bleeding neck
Which miraculously at once began to heal.

Hydra heads whizzed through the air at a terrifying speed,
But Hercules was there to cauterise.
No more heads grew in their places,
No more evil fork-tongued faces,
And at length the Hydra was cut down to size.

So if *you* should meet a Hydra while out walking on the fens,
On no account attempt decapitation.
If you do, you will discover
That the beast will soon recover,
Encouraged by perpetual duplication.

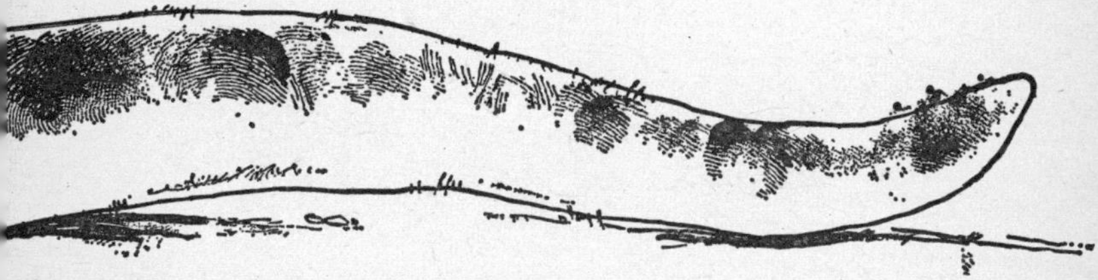

23 Jabberwock

(*A fictitious monster described in the poem 'Jabberwocky' in Lewis Carroll's* Alice Through the Looking-Glass.)

It surely doesn't pay to mock
The bumbling, burbling Jabberwock.
Treat him with deference because
Those biting jaws and snatching claws,
If you insult him or offend,
Will surely get you in the end.
However much you gyre and gimble,
However slithy, mome or nimble,
The Jabberwock will prove your match.
And don't forget the Bandersnatch,
His ally and his greatest pal,
Is equally inimical;
And vorpal blades, so I've been told,
Leave frumious Bandersnatches cold.
So keep away from Jubjub trees
That shelter creatures such as these,
And never make a laughing-stock
Of Lewis Carroll's Jabberwock.

24 King Kong

(A huge monster in the film of that name who was captured and brought back to be put on show in America with disastrous consequences.)

At this monster's demise
There were tears in my eyes
And I sang a most heart-breaking song.
I shall never forget
The first time that we met
When I christened the creature King Kong.

He was big, he was tall,
But that wasn't all,
He was also much harder than teak.
With one crack of his paw
He could shatter your jaw
And lay you out flat for a week.

He lived all alone
On an island unknown
That might never have ever been found,
But our helmsman one night
Got incredibly tight
And we ended up lost and aground.

We scrambled ashore
And set out to explore,
To establish our exact position.
We got into a flap,
For we hadn't a map –
A shockingly careless omission.

The moon was quite bright
So we hunted all night,
Finding nothing but berries and nuts;
But soon it was day
And not far away
We saw several primitive huts.

I gave the command
And our intrepid band
Marched into the compound and halted.
We gave a *s'bonga*
And hammered a gong, a
Procedure that couldn't be faulted.

But no one replied
And it can't be denied
We all felt a strange apprehension.
Though we searched everywhere,
There was nobody there,
And it all seemed to increase the tension.

Signs of life there were none,
For the natives had gone
And we naturally asked ourselves why.
What had caused them to flee?
Had they jumped in the sea?
Or were they incredibly shy?

We discovered that fright
Had occasioned their flight,
For coming towards us we saw
An outsize gorilla
Who looked like a killer,
So we all made a move to withdraw.

But we stopped in alarm
When a long hairy arm
Barred our path and we couldn't escape.
And without further ado
At least three of our crew
Finished up in the mouth of the ape.

All we heard was 'Crunch! Crunch!'
And we all had a hunch
That the beast would be looking for more;
So to frustrate his plan
We turned tail and ran
At a speed never equalled before.

We were soon back aboard
And morale was restored.
(You can't keep down Yankees for long!)
We discussed the huge ape,
His size and his shape;
It was then that I called him King Kong.

We were all well aware
That a creature so rare
Could make millions if handled with skill.
He could make his *début*
In a Broadway revue
And expect to be top of the bill.

Well, to cut my tale short,
(As good raconteurs ought),
With gas shells and nets we gave chase,
And before very long
We captured King Kong
And had him transported to base.

We then sailed away
Without further delay,
With our prisoner chained to the mast.
Sleeping pills in his diet
Kept him peaceful and quiet
And the voyage without incident passed.

After docking we went
To an agent to rent
A theatre on Broadway – 'The Grand' –
Where King Kong could be viewed
Unashamedly nude
In a show we had carefully planned.

Everyone will admit
That King Kong was a hit
And so was his co-star, Fay Wray.
She was Beauty, while he
Played the Beast naturally –
Six evenings and one matinée.

All went well at the start;
Then King Kong lost his heart,
(Though Miss Wray never gave him encouragement).
He broke loose one night,
Grabbed the girl and took flight,
A move that embarrassed the management.

He rushed through the town,
Turning cars upside-down,
Saw the Empire State building ahead;
Climbed right up to the top
And then came to a stop.
(By this time Miss Wray was half-dead.)

King Kong put her down,
Then looked up with a frown
As a fighter plane dived down to get him.
Kong, as it passed by,
Snatched it out of the sky
And plucked out the pilot and ate him!

But to Kong's consternation
More planes in formation
Swept down, firing round after round.
Bullets flew thick and fast
And they got him at last
And he fell with a crash to the ground.

It took ages, I guess,
To clean up the mess
And the blood-stains are there to this day.
His remains slowly rot
In a half-acre plot
With a headstone supplied by Miss Wray.

It runs, 'Here lies King Kong.
It would surely be wrong
And a gross dereliction of duty
If this stone did not state
That it's just tempting fate
When a Beast falls in love with a Beauty.'

25 Kraken

(A mammoth sea-monster, possibly a mile and a half across, sometimes mistaken for an island by unwary sailors.)

The Kraken was a sea-monster two thousand metres wide,
With tentacles that waved about like snakes;
And sometimes weary sailors brought their vessels alongside.
(The Senior Service sometimes makes mistakes.)

The invasion of his privacy the Kraken did not mind;
On the contrary, he welcomed the distraction.
In fact it wasn't often he saw one of his own kind,
So he viewed the anchored ships with satisfaction.

It was when sailors 'stepped ashore' that things got out of hand,
For they thought it was an island they'd located.
They bivouacked and lit their fires on what they thought was land
And the Kraken was well-nigh asphyxiated.

So the Kraken very naturally began to thrash about,
With what Coleridge called 'a short uneasy motion',
And it took the only course it could to put the fires out –
It plunged swiftly to the bottom of the ocean.

Ships and mariners all vanished and were never seen again,
And the lesson to be learned can't be mistaken.
If you anchor near an island in the unfamiliar main,
Just make sure it *is* an island, not a Kraken.

26 Loch Ness Monster

(An elusive water monster reported to be sighted from time to time in Loch Ness.)

When sonsy Scotsmen tak' the route,
They dinna gi'e a tinker's hoot
How rough the way they hae to gang,
Nor if the road is short or lang,
Nor if it costs them mair or less,
If only they avoid Loch Ness;
For there the Monster has her hame,
Beastie of legendary fame.
Naebody's seen her, but they guess she
Would answer to the name of Nessie.
Men fishing in that awesome loch
Swear they have had a nasty shock;
When staring out across the mere,

They say that they have seen appear
A lang thick neck and wee round heid
Wi' ugly phiz to strike one deid.
Lang time ago, the stories say,
A bonny Scot named Jock Macrae
Had filled himself wi' finest malt,
(Started, he couldna call a halt),
Like Blair Athol and Glen McWist,
And Misty Gold and Golden Mist,
And Tangy Heather, Pipers' Joy,
All rounded off wi' Gaelic Boy.
So fou and spoiling for a fight,
When staggering hame one moonlight night,
Loaded wi' whisky to excess,
Jock took a short cut via Loch Ness.
The road for half a mile or more
Followed the gently curving shore.
A lone kirk bell struck twelve o' clock;

The moon was full and so was Jock.
He waved his arms and clenched his fists
And challenged all Welsh Methodists
And Sassenachs and other vermin
To mortal combat to determine
That Scotland's sons were far the best
And in a scrap could beat the rest.
Jock thumped imaginary foes,
Blacked many an e'e, burst many a nose,
And when he'd laid the heathen low
And watched their life-blood freely flow,
On unsure feet, wi' tottering stride
He stumbled to the water's side.
I now must mention – sad confession –
Jock was a poacher by profession.
He'd fished for salmon, trout and bream
In many a sequestrated stream,
And always carried, soon or late,
His rod and line and lots of bait.
Although his movements were unsteady,
Ten minutes later he was ready.
After a final lengthy swig,
Our hero didna' care a fig
If it was morning, noon or night.
Brawlie and gloriously tight,
Befuddled by John Barleycorn,
He would hae confidently sworn
His favourite river flowed before him
Wi outsize salmon waiting for him.
Wi' craft and cunning he was bound
To land one weighing twenty pound.
His first cast could be termed erratic;
His line cracked like an automatic.
He felt a tug, began to wind
And found he'd hooked his kilt behind.
His second cast, by purest chance,
Performed wi' gay exuberance,

Met wi' unusual success,
Shot eighty feet across Loch Ness.
At that same moment Nessie's head
Rose up from off her watery bed;
Her yawning mouth was open wide,
(Jock's hook was buried deep inside).
Her eyes like saucers stared aghast;
Jock thought each moment was his last.
He stared at her in shocked surprise;
He'd never seen a fish that size!
Nor one wi' teeth sae lang and keen,
Nor one whose scales were algal green,
Nor one whose body undulated
And looked distinctly armour-plated,
Wi' ten great humps that arched and curved.
No wonder Jock felt quite unnerved.
At least he knew he'd got a bite
And tugged and pulled wi' all his might,
Hoping to land the biggest fish
That ever graced a supper dish.

For Nessie, too, 'twas quite a shock
To look upon the likes o' Jock,
A hairy Scot fu' to the hilt,
In bonnet blue and gaudy kilt,
Capering about beneath the moon,
Behaving like a crazy loon.
Jock hauled away like Superman,
Convinced he'd caught leviathan,
But Nessie, after one more look,
Snapped off the line that held the hook.
Poor Jock fell flat upon his back
And all his little world went black.
He lay insensible for days,
Lost in an alcoholic haze,
And when restored to fu' sobriety,
Attained a certain notoriety.
According to the local press,
He'd hooked a salmon in Loch Ness!
As for the Monster, down she sank
While Jock was prostrate on the bank.
Mistrustful of the human kind,
She said that she felt disinclined
To leave her underwater caves
To jaup and jink in rippling waves
And sometimes play the giddy goat
To find a hook stuck in her throat.
But later on she found that she
Could not stay, as it were, 'Scotfree'.
She had to leave her watery lair,
Come up to breathe a little air,
And so to-day she's often seen
Like some contorted submarine
Skimming like mad across Loch Ness,
And figures in the local press
As 'Nessie', 'Lug-Ears' or such gammon,
But Jock still swears it was a salmon!

27 Medusa

(One of the three snake-haired Gorgons who turned those who looked at them to stone.)

If invited to tea by Medusa,
Take my tip and politely refuse her.
With one glance alone
She can turn you to stone –
A performance that seems to amuse her.

28 Minotaur

(A hideous creature of Greek legend with the head and horns of a bull and the body of a man, the Minotaur lived in a maze in Crete until it was killed by Theseus.)

The only Minotaur I know
Lived on the Isle of Crete.
Above the waist he was a bull,
A man down to his feet,

Upon his head two monstrous horns,
A hairy slavering snout.
King Minos kept him in a maze
And wouldn't let him out.

The only food he really liked
To eat was human flesh;
His favourite dish a boy or girl
Served best alive and fresh.

Supplies in Crete were running low,
So Minos sailed to Greece
And battered the Athenians
Until they sued for peace.

Apart from paying tribute,
The Athenians had to bring
Seven youths and seven maidens
To Minos every spring.

The hapless youths and maidens
Were pushed inside the maze
To end as lunches, dinners, teas
Served up on out-sized trays.

The Athenian King's son, Theseus,
(Of whom we've heard before),
Decided that the time had come
To slay the Minotaur.

His father said, 'One thing, my son,
The vessel's sails are black.
If you succeed, change them to white
To show you're coming back.'

Theseus replied, 'You know me, Dad.
I've never known defeat.
I'll change the sails from black to white
When I come home from Crete.'

With six more youths and seven maids
Young Theseus sailed the sea,
Reporting to King Minos
At exactly half-past three.

'We've got an hour,' King Minos said,
'Before we feed the beast;
And on occasions such as this
We hold a special feast.'

He led them to the banquet hall
And Theseus took his seat
Alongside Minos' daughter
Who looked good enough to eat.

Her name was Ariadne
And she liked the boy from Greece.
She planned to get him from the maze
Alive and in one piece.

When Minos wasn't looking,
Before the meal was through,
She slipped the Greek a ball of wool
And a magic broadsword too.

After the feast was over,
The Greeks were pushed inside
The labyrinth where the Minotaur
Had chosen to reside.

With the wool tied to the door-post,
Gripping the magic blade,
Young Theseus pressed on all alone,
Resolved and unafraid.

Unwinding wool as he advanced
By many devious ways,
Our hero found himself at last
In the centre of the maze.

And there he saw the Minotaur,
Ugliest of combatants,
Whose bellowings almost caused the Greek
To leap out of his pants.

The monster charged at Theseus,
Horns ominously lowered,
But Theseus nimbly stepped aside
And used his magic sword.

He plunged it in the creature's neck;
The magic did its stuff.
The Minotaur, quite out of breath,
Had clearly had enough.

Young Theseus waited to make sure
The beast was really dead;
Then found the entrance to the maze
By following the thread.

Theseus and his companions
Set out at once for home;
With Ariadne safe aboard,
They sped across the foam.

If Theseus had changed the sail,
All would have finished sound,
But he forgot and so his Dad
Jumped off a cliff and drowned.

The story of the Minotaur
Is anything but dull,
But I confess that it contains
A little too much bull!

29 Polyphemus

(One of the giant Cyclopes who lived in Sicily. One-eyed, he was blinded by Odysseus.)

Polyphemus was a giant who had one enormous eye.
(Odysseus, art thou plotting there below?)
According to the legends he was fifty cubits high.
(A cubit's one foot six, as we all know.)
He was something of a glutton.
Living by and large on mutton,
For he had a flock of sixty sheep or so.

He lived upon an island not a thousand miles from Troy.
(Odysseus, art thou lost upon the wave?)
He had started his career as just a simple shepherd boy
And had settled down inside a mountain cave,
Where he led a peaceful life,
For he hadn't got a wife;
Every obol that he earned he used to save.

Zigzagging on the ocean came a fleet of weary Greeks.
(Odysseus, art thou squinting at thy map?)
They'd been hoping for a land-fall for weeks and weeks and weeks,
And Odysseus was clearly in a flap;
And to aggravate their passions
They were running short of rations.
Every man aboard was spoiling for a scrap.

When they saw the Cyclops' island every sailor raised a cheer.
(Odysseus, art thou steering by the sun?)
'No sign of life,' their leader said. 'We'll play it all by ear.
A recce is the first thing to be done.'
He assured each volunteer
He himself would guard the rear.
If they *were* attacked, he'd be their champion.

So they landed on the island and they started to explore.
(Odysseus, art thou shivering with fright?)
In their foolishness they fancied that Odysseus knew the score;
After all, they weren't particularly bright.
When they saw the cave, he cried,
'Don't be nervous. Step inside.
This adventure, just for once, will be all right.'

In the cave they found some cheeses, bowls of milk and woolly ewes.
(Odysseus, art thou ready for a shock?)
They danced for joy, then ate and drank, and started to enthuse
When they saw the size of Polyphemus' stock.
Then they heard the tramp of feet,
Lots of baas and many a bleat.
It was Polyphemus driving home his flock.

They began to curse their leader when they saw the giant's size.
(Odysseus, art thou shaking like a leaf?)
The bleak prospect each envisaged was a premature demise.
Long ago they'd stopped relying on their chief.
So resolved to do or die,
They looked Cyclops in the eye.
From Odysseus they expected no relief.

They were even more disturbed when Polyphemus grabbed two men;
(Odysseus, art thou really a creep?)
Ate them without salt or pepper; sealed the entrance to his den
With a rock, and then he promptly fell asleep.
Odysseus, skulking in the rear,
Quite beside himself with fear,
Heard his sailors all begin to wail and weep.

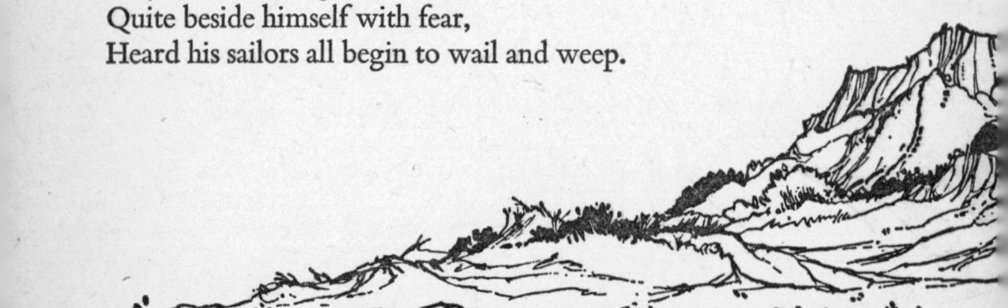

In times of stress man always finds a last shot in his locker.
(Odysseus, art thou supplicating Zeus?)
The Grecian chief evolved a plan that really was a shocker
And he very quickly put it into use.
First he found a wooden stake
That would neither bend nor break.
(Why he wanted it most readers will deduce.)

One end of it he whittled down as sharp as any skewer.
(Odysseus, thou art not so dumb a guy.)
Then he fanned the giant's fire to the hottest temperature;
Thrust the stake in. Yes, you've guessed the reason why!
Once the tip was black and charred
By the flames, it grew rock-hard;
So he poked it straight in Polyphemus' eye.

Polyphemus shrieked in agony and galloped round and round,
(Odysseus, art thou kneeling down to pray?)
Staggered blindly to the exit and sat down upon the ground
With his back against the rock to bar the way.
So the Greeks were in despair,
Prisoners in the giant's lair;
Every sailor eyed Odysseus with dismay.

In the morning Polyphemus pushed the massive rock aside,
(Odysseus, art thou wondering what to do?)
And the air inside the cave was not exactly rarefied;
There's no doubt it would have turned red litmus blue.
In a line his woolly flock
Slipped between him and the rock,
Each one longing for lush grass and morning dew.

Now crafty Polyphemus knew the Greeks were full of guile,
(Odysseus, art thou feeling rather cocky?)
So he felt the back of each sheep as they passed in single file
Just in case one had an unofficial jockey.
But Odysseus had a scheme
And it worked just like a dream,
Even though his men were heavy, broad and stocky.

He instructed every sailor to hang on *beneath* a beast.
(Odysseus, art thou hanging on as well?)
It's obvious that the animals were adequately fleeced
For not a single 'easy rider' fell.
So the Greeks down to this day
Talk of those that got away
From a super-Cyclopean sentinel!

30 Pterodactyl

(A flying reptile with a wing span of over six metres. Fortunately it is now extinct.)

Please ptell me, Pterodactyl,
Who ptaught you how pto fly?
Who ptaught you how pto flap your wings
And soar up in the sky?

No prehistoric monster
Could ptake off just like you
And pturn and ptwist and ptaxi
Way up there in the blue.

Pray ptell me, Pterodactyl,
Just how you spent your day.
What were your favourite hobbies?
Did you gather nuts in May?

Did you ever throw a nimble dart,
Ptry Karate or Kung-Fu,
Or ptake up stamp-collecting,
Or paddle a canoe?

Were you ever a numismatist,
A ptenderfoot or scout?
Did you join the local chess club?
Did you ever ptickle ptrout?

Did you sometimes perch in ptree-ptops,
Beech or oak or sycamore?
Did the branch snap off and did you
Crash down on the forest floor?

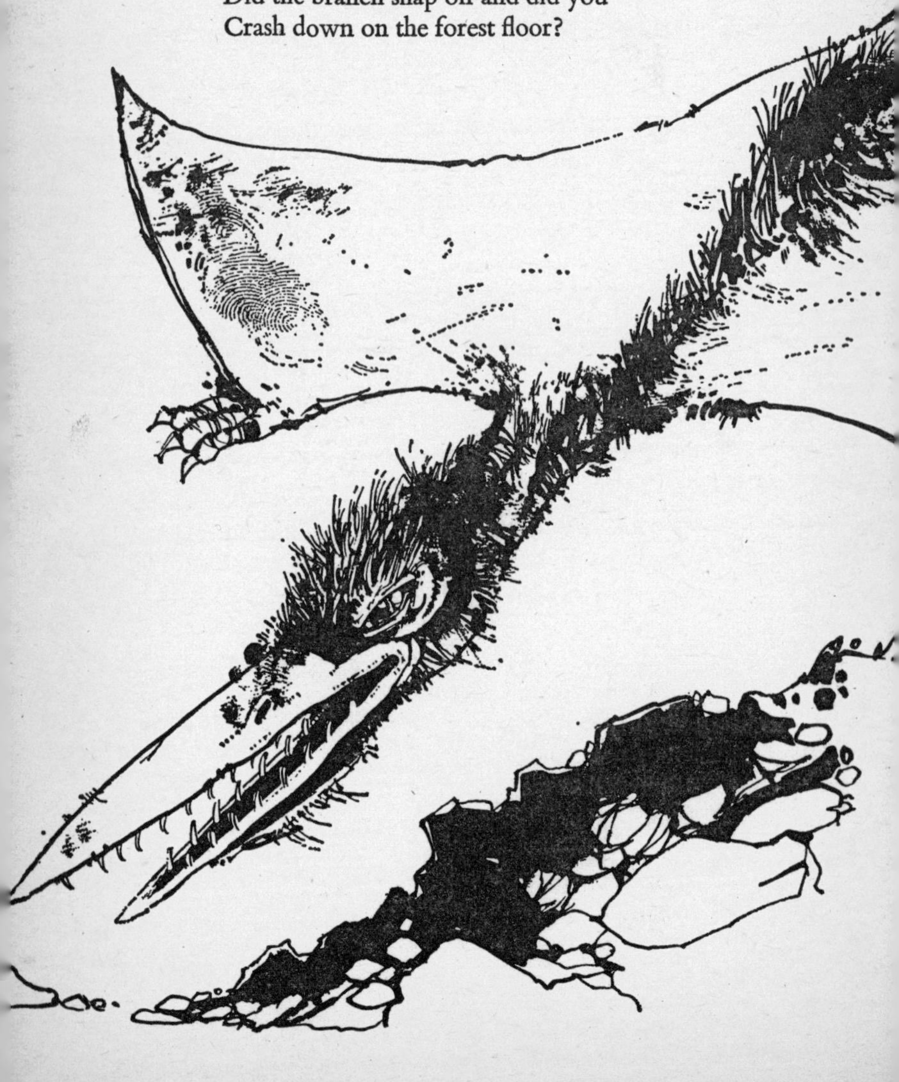

Were you bird or were you lizard?
Ptell me that at least I beg.
And one final thing I ask you –
Did you ever lay an egg?

On one count I must reproach you;
You are difficult pto spell,
Worse than ptarmigan or ptom-ptit.
(Silent 'p's' make spelling hell!)

31 Roc

(*A giant bird, with a wing span of thirty or so paces, encountered by Sindbad the Sailor in* The Arabian Nights' Entertainments.)

You all know of Sindbad the Sailor,
Of his exploits and fabulous quests,
But you may not have heard
How he once got the bird
And frequented the strangest of nests.

For some weeks he had sailed round in circles,
(His helmsman was feeling depressed).
With commendable zeal
Sindbad grabbed at the wheel
And steered north by east by north-west.

Unmanned by this change in direction,
The sailors all rushed to the prow.
Sindbad blinked with surprise,
Scarce believing his eyes.
There was land on the starboard bow!

The coast looked completely deserted;
Sindbad headed the ship for the beach.
It soon ran aground;
Then the crew gathered round
For their captain's traditional speech.

'We have braved many dangers together,
The dark clouds have now quite disappeared –'
Sindbad paused for effect
And to show their respect
The men touched their forelocks and cheered.

Sindbad opened his mouth to continue,
But before he could get out a word,
The crew started to shout
As the sky was blacked out
By a hovering gigantic bird.

Its wings spanned the sky up above them
And flapped like the cracks of a whip.
The crew, quite out of hand,
Scrambled down on the sand,
Abandoning captain and ship.

Sindbad, howling abuse as they scattered,
Called each one a mutinous swab,
Left to fight for his life,
Put an edge on his knife
And a point on his thingumabob.

The sight of the bird up above him
To Sindbad had not been a shock.
He had heard of its fame
And he knew that its name
In the text-books was simply the Roc.

A Roc-bird could pick up and carry,
He recalled with a good deal of awe,
(So strong were its wings)
Among other things
Two elephants, one in each claw.

The Roc settled down on the poop-deck.
Sindbad nervously fingered his knife,
But he had an idea
He had nothing to fear,
For the bird was not seeking his life.

In fact the Roc looked rather woeful,
Tears suddenly rolled down its cheek,
And it screwed up its face
In a tragic grimace
As they dripped from the end of its beak.

By signs and with eloquent gestures
At last the Roc's message got through.
Sindbad clung to its neck
As it shot off the deck
And rocketed into the blue.

The Roc and its intrepid rider
Flew south by south-east by south-west,
And there in a glade
Was the biggest egg laid,
In surely the biggest of nests.

From the bird's most expressive sign-language
Sindbad learned why the Roc looked forlorn.
The egg shell was so thick
That the poor little chick
Couldn't peck its way out and get born!

Sindbad climbed in the nest and got stabbing,
Attacking the egg shell with zest.
He thrust with his knife,
Hacked away for dear life;
The shell cracked and the chick did the rest!

The Roc proudly gazed on its offspring,
Said his wife always wanted a son.
First he drank Sindbad's health,
Then he showered him with wealth,
Just to thank him for all he had done.

He then flew him back to his vessel;
(The crew had returned to the ship.)
There were tears in all eyes
As they waved their goodbyes
Before starting the long homeward trip.

For years after, if sailors were shipwrecked
On that distant identical coast,
Any Roc that was sighted
Was more than delighted
To play the hospitable host.

32 Scylla

(A nymph who was turned into a monster by Circe. Thereafter she lived in the sea between Sicily and Italy and was a danger to mariners.)

Between Reggio and Messina there's a narrow strip of sea
Which, as far as shipping goes, is quite a killer.
On the one side is Charybdis and exactly vis-à-vis
Is the monster known to classicists as Scylla.

Now if Homer wasn't nodding, Scylla had a dozen feet,
(Which meant she wore at least six pairs of boots),
And as far as heads went, though she could with Cerberus
compete,
The Hydra had the edge, no one disputes.

But the Scylla's heads, the legends say, had teeth in three grim rows
And every tooth was sharp and full of bane,
So every ship that sailed within a mile or two of those
Was swallowed up and never seen again.

So if you *must* negotiate that doubly dangerous strait,
Make sure you have an expert at the tiller,
For if Charybdis doesn't get you, rest assured that soon or late
You will fall a victim to six-headed Scylla.

33 Sphinx

(The Egyptian Sphinx had the body of a lion and the head of a man or ram, while the Grecian Sphinx had the body of a lion with wings, the head of a woman and the tail of a serpent.)

The Egyptian Sphinx says little
That we can understand;
Half-man, half-lion, there he lies
Half-buried in the sand.

His reputation wholly rests,
As far as I can see,
On his impassive mien and cool
Inscrutability.

The Egyptian Sphinx says, 'Ma 'lêsh!'[1]
'Ibnek fên?'[2] and 'Kêf hâlkum?'[3]
He wears a tasselled tarboosh
And is 'akbar kulluhum!'[4]

The Grecian Sphinx has other traits
And quite a different life-style;
A lion's body, female's head
And wings that keep it mobile.

She will also ask a riddle;
If your answer is correct,
Then your worries are all over;
You are one of the elect.

But if you cannot tell her
Why a door is not a door,
Or why chickens cross the roadway,
Or why two and two make four,
Why a raven's like a writing-desk,
Or why the bull should rush,
Or why on earth the brandy snaps,
Or why the bell should push,
Or why the sea is boiling hot,
Or whether pigs have wings,
Or where flies go in winter-time,
Or why the Highland flings,
Then I greatly fear you've had it,
You are doomed beyond recall,
For she'll either hurl you off a cliff
Or devour you, bones and all!

1 No matter 2 Where is your son? 3 How are you? 4 Greatest of all

34 Unicorn

(A fabulous creature with the body of a horse and a single horn believed to have magical and medicinal properties.)

When hunting for the Unicorn,
Look for its single twisted horn,
White, black and red and four feet long
And so exceptionally strong
No other beast dare venture out
If there's a unicorn about.
Lions and tigers quake with fear
If any Unicorn is near;
All jungle creatures puff and pant,
And that includes the elephant.
If man with Unicorn should strive,
There's little doubt which will survive.
And that is why I want to warn
All those who hunt the Unicorn
There's only one technique, I guess,
That's guaranteed to bring success.

If you do everything I say,
You'll live to fight another day.

Together with a virgin maid
Seek out some quiet secluded glade,
Garland the girl with flowers, then she
Must sit and wait beneath a tree,
While you are lurking very near
To watch the Unicorn appear.
You'll hear it stamp and roar and snort,
Curvet and gallop, then stop short,
And next you'll be amazed to see
The Unicorn respectfully
Bow down before your maiden bait
And gracefully capitulate.
Now, while the beast is hypnotised,
You'll find that it can be surprised,
So armed with net or snare or gin,
It's up to you to dash right in.
The Unicorn, (so legends tell),
Is held fast in a curious spell.
Attack it with exuberance
While it is helpless in this trance.

The value of the Unicorn
Lies in its quaintly crumpled horn.
All would-be murderers agree
It has one useful property.
So if you're driven to homicide
And bored with common cyanide,
This creature's horn, if powdered fine
And sprinkled in a glass of wine,
Gives plonk a far more lethal kick
Than strychnine or than arsenic.

(The powder's also efficacious
With meats or dishes farinaceous.)

35 Wendigo

(*A huge, indeterminate flying creature described in a story by Algernon Blackwood in his* Tales of the Uncanny and Supernatural.)

It was autumn in the forest,
And the leaves were at their brownest,
And the trees were at their tallest,
And the lakes were at their wettest
On that sunny autumn morning,
On that morning in the autumn.
And the squawking of the widgeon,
And the fluting of the Fluff-bird,
And the whistle of the windfinch,
All these noises reached the wigwam
Of the doughty Hiawatha
Who was sleeping on his ground-sheet
Made of subtly chosen skunk-skins.
Minnehaha lay beside him,
Minnehaha, Giggling Liquid,
Minnehaha, his beloved,
In her nightdress edged with wampum,
Edged with yards and yards of wampum.

All the noises of the forest,
Squawking, fluting, whistling, booming,
Woke the mighty Hiawatha
And the gentle Minnehaha.
Then, while Minnie cooked the breakfast,
Hiawatha donned his head-dress
Gaudy with the choicest feathers
Of the Yellow-spotted Field-twit,
Haunter of the bogs and marshes;
Next slipped on his fur-lined long johns,
Afterwards his purple corduroys
And his moccasins of lamb's-wool;
Finally his leather tunic
Studded in the latest fashion,
Silver studs to form a message,
Simple message in block letters
Reading, *H. LOVES MINNEHAHA*.

Hiawatha took his arrows,
Sharpened them with keen-edged bowie,
Seized his bow of pliant willow,
Went out hunting while his Missus
Built a fire of twigs and fir-cones
And some sheets of *Ideal Wigwam*
Sprinkled well with lighter fuel
To get the conflagration started.
Then she hunted in the larder,
Found some strips of fatty bacon,
Three tomatoes and a duck egg,
But she chose a pair of kippers,
Hiawatha's favourite fishes,
Placed them in a pan for frying,
Added lumps of rancid butter
Just to give the dish a flavour,
Set the pan down on the embers,
Watched the contents spit and simmer,
While she waited for her husband
To come home and have his breakfast.

Meanwhile in the darksome forest
Underneath the rustling pine trees,
Hiawatha moved with caution,
Hoping to track down a bison
Which would serve for Sunday's dinner,
Or an elk or moose or reindeer,
Any creature that would furnish
Fillet steak or rump or sirloin
For his personal consumption
And scrag-ends for Minnehaha.

Suddenly he saw a footprint,
Saw a footprint in a clearing,
Studied it with some amazement,
For its size was truly startling,
While its shape was far from human.
On the other hand, no creature
Ever seen by Hiawatha
Could have left a print so monstrous –
Eighteen inches long it measured
And its width was fourteen inches.
Hiawatha also noticed
That the giant print was blood-stained
And the grass was burnt and blackened.

Then at last it dawned upon him
As he looked down at the footmark,
He was suffering from delusions,
For although his keen eyes covered
All the ground within the clearing,
He could see no other footprint.
Then he came to the conclusion
That the animal that made it
Must have hopped there from the bushes,
Hopped there from beneath the pine trees,
Then hopped back a little later;
Hence the solitary footprint.

Hiawatha left the clearing,
Made ten paces through the forest,
Through the silent awesome forest;
Then he saw another footprint
Very similar to the first one,
Just as huge and just as blood-stained,
Just as puzzling, just as baffling,
And indeed the only difference
Was the first print was the right foot,
While the second was the left foot!

Hiawatha did not panic,
Though he logically reasoned
If he'd stumbled on the footprints
Of some unknown forest creature
That had passed that way before him,
He was on the track of something
Rarely seen but sometimes mentioned,
Mentioned by his fellow-Indians,
Only spoken of in whispers,

Called by some Sasquatch or Big-Foot
And the Wendigo by others.

On the trail stalked Hiawatha,
Ill equipped to fight a monster,
Just a knife and bow and arrows
And a lariat made of wampum
Were his sole means of protection.
He advanced some twenty paces;
Then he saw another footprint,
Long and broad and very blood-stained,
So he had no doubt whatever
That the Wendigo was lurking
Somewhere in the lonesome forest,
Hidden in the leafy tree-tops,
Waiting to reach down and grab him,
Bear him off to grace the menu
At some Wendigo-ish banquet;
For his grandmother had told him
That the Wendigo was partial
To an Indian, stewed and roasted.

Though a brave, our crafty hero
Called to mind the Indian proverb
That the better part of valour
Has a flavour of discretion,
So he there and then decided
To return to Minnehaha,
Seek the safety of his wigwam,
Hide beneath a stack of wampum,
Leave his tracking and his hunting
Till the Wendigo had travelled
Further north to plague the Blackfeet,
Or the Pawnees or the Hurons,
Or the Rabbit-Teeth or Chipmunks,
The Apaches or Ojibways,
Any tribe but Hiawatha's.

As he stumbled through the forest,
Hiawatha heard above him
Something rushing through the tree-tops
Like the whistling wind of winter,
And the sound increased in volume
To a melancholy howling
Like the wailing of a banshee,
Like the love-song of a tom-cat,
And the forest seemed to darken
And close in on Hiawatha
Till he could not see before him
And ran smack into a fir-tree.
At that very self-same moment
A mysterious something gripped him,
Took a firm hold of his wampum,
Whisked him out of this dimension,
Flew with him across the heavens
At a speed that was alarming,
For his clothes were singed and smouldering
And his wampum, too, was burning.

Luckily for Hiawatha,
Just before he reached the moment
Of spontaneous combustion,
His most curious captor dropped him,
Dropped him into Gitche Gumee,
In the Shining Big-Sea Water,
Not too distant from his wigwam,
Where his darling Minnehaha
Was still busy with his breakfast,
With the kippers she was cooking.

And when Hiawatha told her
That the Wendigo had seized him,
Borne him far across the forest
At a hundred miles a minute
And incontinently dropped him
With a splash in Gitche Gumee,
Minnehaha simply giggled,
Urged him to cut down his drinking,
Begged him to keep off the bottle
For he couldn't hold his liquor.

Afterwards at celebrations
Such as birthdays or engagements,
Wedding feasts or family christenings,
When the wine was flowing freely,
Minnehaha, full of mischief,
Would sneak up on Hiawatha
Every time he grabbed a cocktail,
And before he even sipped it
She would whisper just to tease him,
'Do not touch it, Hiawatha!
Stick to squash or bitter lemon,
Lest the demon drink confuse you,
Lest the Wendigo should get you!'

36 Werewolf

(A man changed into a wolf at the time of the new moon, the werewolf can be killed only by a silver bullet.)

A Werewolf is just like a wolf –
Long teeth, slavering tongue, bristling hair –
But a wolf can be dated, is easily located,
While a werewolf is simply not there.

A wolf can be found on the steppes,
Chasing Russian, troika or bear;
But if you're on the track of a Werewolf, alack,
It will drive you to abject despair.

A wolf's a predictable beast;
It proceeds in a certain direction,
While a Werewolf will say, 'I'll be with you to-day',
But it never turns up for inspection.

A wolf feeds whenever it can
On chicken or rabbit or hare;
But a Werewolf, they say, likes to eat twice a day
And prefers human flesh, medium rare.

Some men, when the moon's at the full,
Undergo a complete transformation;
With fierce howls and roars, they run round on all fours,
Killing people without hesitation.

When they turn into Werewolves themselves,
Their nails grow much sharper and longer;
When their palms become hairy, then it's best to be wary,
For the odds are they're now getting stronger.

If ever you meet with a Werewolf,
Remember this piece of advice –
A real silver bullet, fired straight down its gullet,
Will finish it off in a trice.

37 Wyvern

(A sort of flying serpent, rather like a dragon, with two eagles' legs and a barbed tail.)

All my research has shown
Very little is known
Of the Wyvern or where it inhabits;
One informant insists
That the creature exists
Upon rhubarb, rice pudding and rabbits.

I also have heard
That the Wyvern's a bird
Reminiscent of serpent or snake;
It has two eagle's legs
And it lays speckled eggs
That young ornithologists take.

Of incredible size,
Like a dragon that flies,
With a wing span of twenty-five feet,
The Wyvern is not
Any problem to pot,
And when roasted is pleasant to eat.

Its long-taloned claws
And its slavering jaws
Are features entirely distinct.
Big-game hunters who chase it
Can outwit and outpace it,
And maybe that's why it's extinct!

38 Yeti

(Also known as the Abominable Snowman, the Yeti is a huge hairy creature that is said to inhabit the dense forests high on the slopes of the Himalayas.)

It was an ancient Sherpa-man
Who told the tale to me.
'By my snow-white beard and piercing eye,
In my life I've seen but three.

'The Yeti that I first espied
Was lug-eared, lank and lean,
His oval head was brownish-red,
His ape-like face obscene.

'His hairy body was so vile
It filled me full of fear.
Completely nude, he looked quite rude
Both from the front and rear.

'He had long arms, was seven feet tall,
His footprints looked like craters;
His skin was rough and very tough
Just like an alligator's.

'I met him in a narrow pass
Up in remote Tibet.
I kept my head and simply said,
"I'm please to meet you", yet –

'Before I could complete the word,
The creature turned quite white,
Gibbered and squeaked, then promptly streaked
Till it was out of sight.

'Searching for yetis after that
Became for me compulsive;
I wondered why they were so shy.
Did *they* find *us* repulsive?

'Perhaps they rated you and me
Inadequately hairy.
The pale smooth face of the human race
To them was rather scary.

'My second Yeti hunt was backed
By Barnum, famous showman.
Vast wealth I'd get if I could net
An Abominable Snowman.

'I sought him here, I sought him there,
I climbed up Everest.
For weeks I searched, then found him perched
Upon a mountain crest.

'This time I did not make a sound,
Just eyed him from below.
An hour at least I watched the beast
A-squatting in the snow.

'At length he sighed quite plaintively
Three times or maybe four;
His eyelids closed, then off he dozed
With many a tell-tale snore.

'I crept up quietly on my toes,
Holding my net on high.
I felt no fear as I drew near,
Resolved to do or die.

'I brought the net down with a swish,
But in the fading light
I muffed my stroke; the Yeti woke
And swung round, full of fight.

'There comes a time when each man must
Do what he's got to do.
I counted "one" and thereupon
Strategically withdrew.

'My third and final Yeti hunt
Was in remote Tibet,
Travelling as far as Shangri-La
By supersonic jet.

'At last in a lamasery
I tracked that Yeti down.
To dodge his fate he'd shaved his pate
And donned a yellow gown.

‘The other monks were five feet two,
But he was ten feet four.
There was no doubt that he stood out
Like the proverbial thumb that’s sore.

‘A giant among leprechauns,
He towered above the rest.
I realised at once that I’d
Come on a hopeless quest.

‘I knew that Yeti had me licked
In normal rough and tumble,
But whose would be the victory
In contests far more humble?

‘I thought of billiards and darts,
Of dominoes and euchre,
Of cribbage, nap, poker and snap;
I even thought of snooker.

‘I thought of games both high and low,
Of games both more and less;
And then I knew just what to do –
I challenged him at chess.

‘To my surprise the Yeti smiled
Inscrutably and stated
He’d sail with me across the sea
If he should be checkmated,

‘But if *he* won, then I must swear
Without any reservation
To mend my ways and spend my days
In Yeti preservation.

'I'll never know what I did wrong,
Or what I didn't do,
Nor how my play went quite astray
Though brilliant hitherto.

'I moved the White King's Bishop's Pawn
Two squares decisively.
The Yeti sighed and then replied
With King's Pawn to King Three.

'I promptly seized my King's Knight's Pawn
And moved it to Knight Four,
Following a plan that Capablan –
– Ca might have used before.

'The Yeti gently steered his Queen
To King's Rook Five and cried,
"Admit it, do! That's mate in two!
It cannot be denied."

'From that day on I've roamed the world,
Passing from land to land,
Preaching to all, both short and tall,
In words they understand.

'I ask all yeti-hunting men
To try their luck elsewhere;
Urge them to aim at other game,
Like tiger, lynx or bear,

'Or elephant, or crocodile,
Or even spermaceti,
And all because one day I was
Fool's-mated by a Yeti.'

More Beaver Books

We hope you have enjoyed this Beaver Book. Here are some of the other titles:

The Beaver Book of Horror A Beaver original. Daniel Farson's journey into the mysterious world of ghosts, vampires, werewolves, killer cats, monsters and zombies, illustrated with black and white photographs

Junket and Jumbles A Beaver original. A delightful collection of funny verse – rhymes, riddles, limericks and tongue-twisters – chosen by Raymond Wilson and illustrated by Russell Coulson

Storm Warning A powerful novel for older readers set in pre-war Nazi Germany, about a young English girl who helps two Jewish children escape from the Gestapo. By Mara Kay

Covens and Cauldrons An anthology of stories, folk tales, poems and legends about witches, edited by Jacynth Hope-Simpson and strikingly illustrated by Krystyna Turska

Looking at Wildlife A Beaver original. Nicholas Hammond has written an invaluable guide for young naturalists, with lots of information on all kinds of wild creatures as well as advice on the best ways of observing them. Illustrated throughout

Time's Delights A Beaver original. A collection of poems old and new about all aspects of time, chosen by Raymond Wilson, with enchanting illustrations by Meg Rutherford

New Beavers are published every month and if you would like the *Beaver Bulletin* – which gives all the details – please send a large stamped addressed envelope to:

Beaver Bulletin
The Hamlyn Group
Astronaut House
Feltham
Middlesex TW14 9AR

362981